D1029002

WRITTEN BY JODY JENSEN SHAFFER ILLUSTRATED BY TERESA ALBERINI

INSIDE MY BODY

HEART

PARK

ONE-WAY

MOST AMAZING MUSCLE

amicus illustrated

Amicus Illustrated is published by Amicus
P.O. Box 1329, Mankato, MN 56002
www.amicuspublishing.us

Library of Congress Cataloging-in-Publication Data
Shaffer, Jody Jensen, author.
 My heart / by Jody Jensen Shaffer ; Illustrated by
Teresa Alberini.
    pages cm. — (Inside my body) (Amicus illustrated)
 Summary: "After getting their heart rates up while
on a bike ride, a boy named Rico teaches his younger
sister Rosa about the heart"—Provided by publisher.
 Audience: K to grade 3.
 ISBN 978-1-60753-755-7 (library binding) —
ISBN 978-1-60753-854-7 (ebook)
1. Heart—Juvenile literature. 2. Human physiology—
Juvenile literature. I. Alberini, Teresa, illustrator.
II. Title.
 QP111.6.S46 2016
 612.1'7—dc23   2014041500

Editor: Rebecca Glaser
Designer: Kathleen Petelinsek

Printed in the United States of America at
Corporate Graphics in North Mankato, Minnesota.

10 9 8 7 6 5 4 3 2 1

ABOUT THE AUTHOR

Jody Jensen Shaffer is the author of 19
books of fiction and nonfiction for children.
She also writes poetry, stories, and articles
in children's magazines. She tries to keep
her body healthy by walking regularly and
eating nutritious foods. Visit Jody on the
web at jodyjensenshaffer.blogspot.com.

ABOUT THE ILLUSTRATOR

Teresa Alberini has always loved painting
and drawing. She attended the Academy
of Fine Arts in Florence, Italy, and she now
lives and works as an illustrator in a small
town on the Italian coast. Visit her on the
web at www.teresaalberini.com.

"I have to stop, Rosa. My tire has a leak."

"I'm going to sit. I'm tired, Rico!"

"My heart is tired, too. That hill was steep!"

"My legs are tired. Not my heart."

"Your heart's been pumping, too. Feel your wrist."

"My wrist?"

"You can feel your heart beat there. It's called your pulse. It tells how fast your heart's pumping. We learned about it in health class."

"My heart's beating fast!"

"Mine too."

"When I'm sleeping, could someone feel my pulse?"

"Yes. But they might wake you up!"

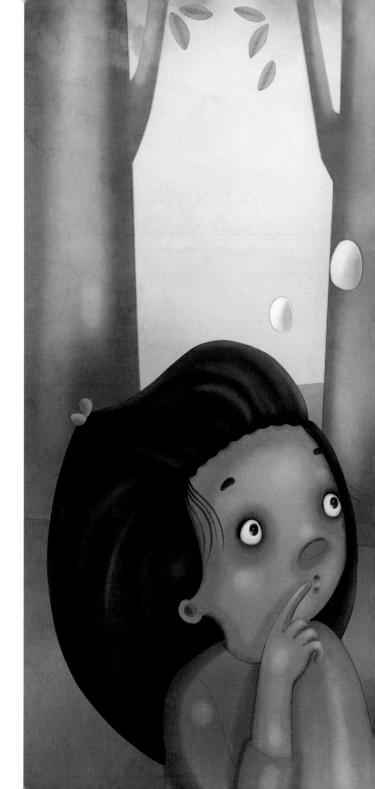

"Your heart beats all the time. You don't have to think about it. When you sleep, your heart slows down, and your blood moves more slowly."

"Blood? Aren't we talking about my heart, Rico?"

"You can't talk about one without the other. Your heart's job is to pump blood."

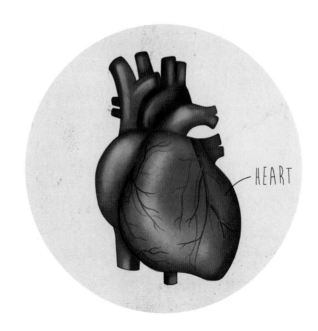

HEART

"But what does blood do?"

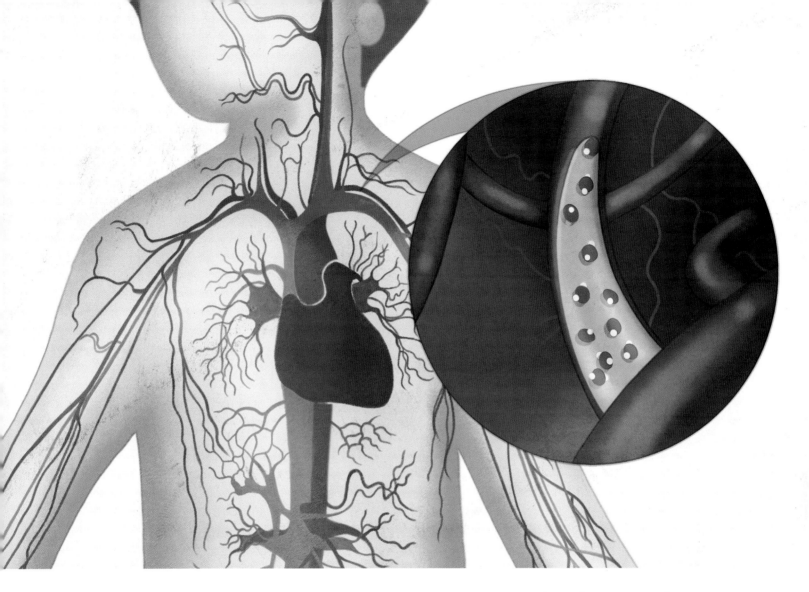

"Blood delivers everything your body needs:
the oxygen you breathe in and nutrients from
food to give you energy."

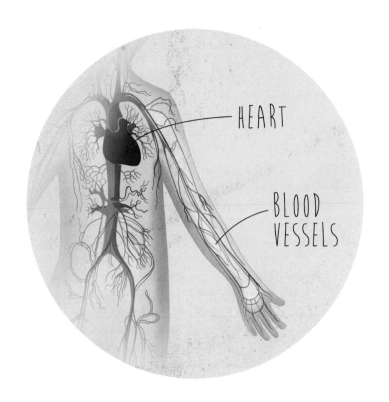

HEART

BLOOD VESSELS

"So how does the heart pump blood around my body, Rico?"

"Blood travels in thin tubes called blood vessels. Blood vessels connect your heart with other parts of your body—like the bike paths connect places in the city."

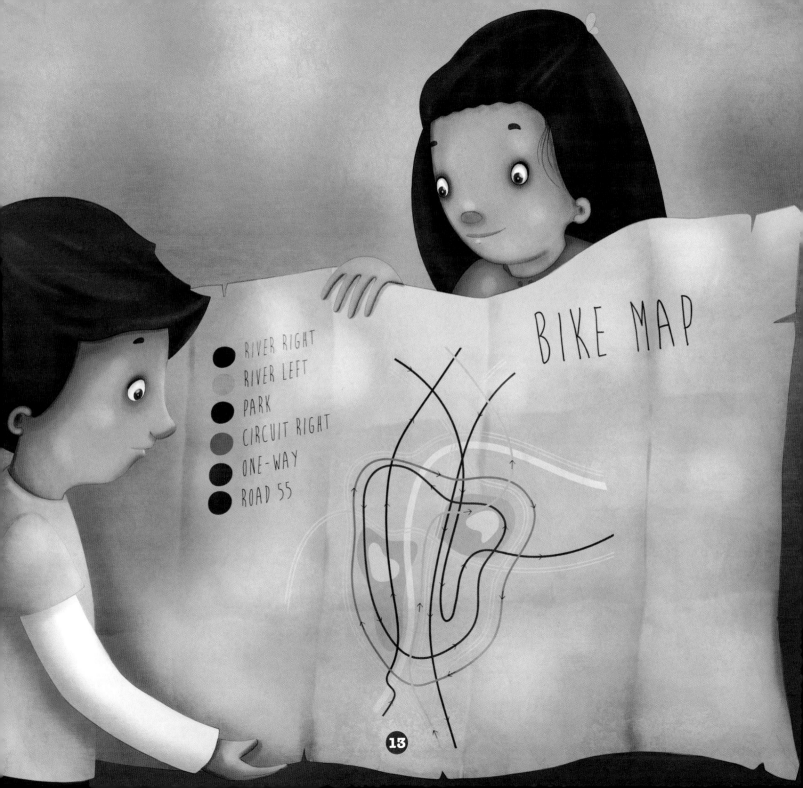

"Some of the paths are one-ways."

"So are blood vessels, Rosa. Arteries only take blood away from your heart. That blood has oxygen in it. Then veins bring blood back to your heart, after the oxygen and nutrients are used up."

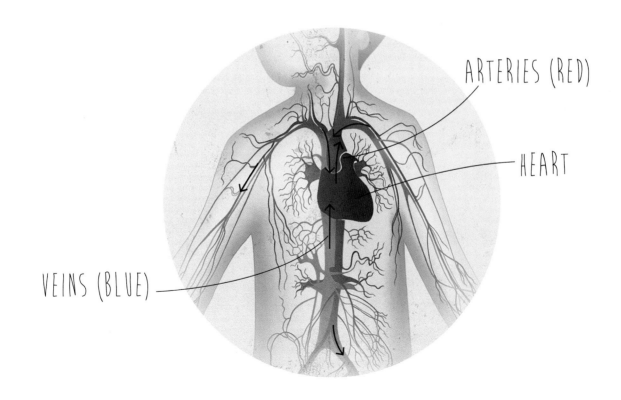

ARTERIES (RED)

HEART

VEINS (BLUE)

"What about when my blood leaks out? Like last week when I skinned my knee?"

"There are tiny blood vessels close to your skin, called capillaries. They break and bleed when you get a scrape."

"My heart was beating really fast, too, Rico."

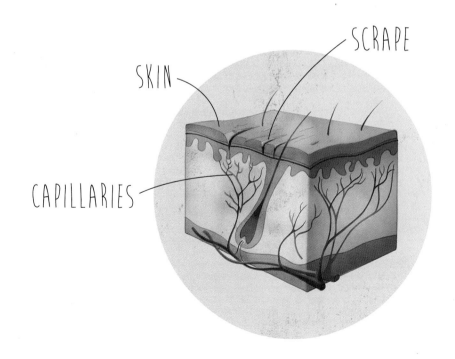

SKIN

SCRAPE

CAPILLARIES

17

"That's because your heart speeds up when you exercise or get scared."

"How fast is it supposed to beat?"

"Seventy to 110 times a minute when you're resting."

"Doesn't my heart get tired?"

"Your heart's an amazing muscle, Rosa. It pumps without stopping until you die."

"It must be huge!"

"It's about the size of your fist. But it's the most important muscle in your body. Without it, you'd die."

"I hope mine lasts a long time!"

"Well, eating healthy food helps your heart."

"What about exercise, Rico?"

"That too. Riding home will be good exercise!"

BODY BY THE NUMBERS

Heart 1

Lungs 2

Arteries, Veins, and Capillaries
All of your blood vessels stretched out would be more than 60,000 miles (96,560 km) long!

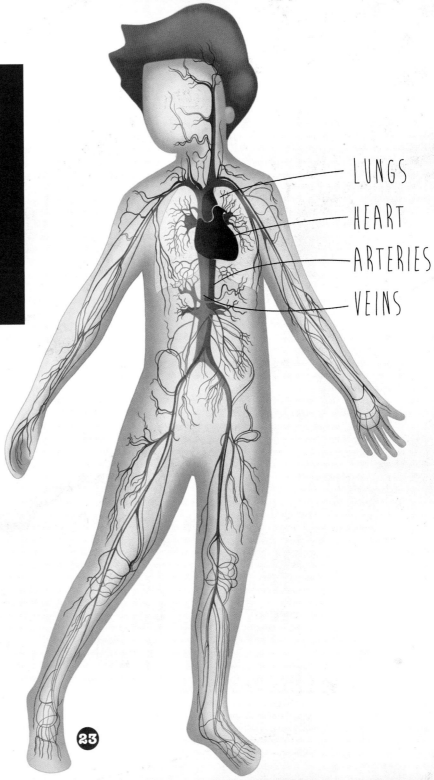

LUNGS

HEART

ARTERIES

VEINS

23

GLOSSARY

artery—A tube that takes oxygen-rich blood from your heart to your body.

blood vessels—Large and small tubes that carry blood, oxygen, and nutrients in your body.

capillary—The smallest type of artery in your body; the capillaries closest to your skin are the ones that break when you get a scrape.

heart—The muscle in your chest that pumps blood around your body.

pulse—The throbbing of the arteries as your heart pumps blood through them.

vein—A tube that carries oxygen-poor blood from your body to your heart.

READ MORE

Corcoran, Mary K. **The Circulatory Story**. Watertown, Mass.: Charlesbridge, 2010.

Leigh, Autumn. **The Circulatory System**. New York: Gareth Stevens, 2012.

Halvorson, Karin. **Inside the Heart**. Minneapolis: ABDO Publishing, 2013.

WEBSITES

The Children's University of Manchester: The Heart
www.childrensuniversity.manchester.ac.uk/interactives/science/exercise/heart/
See a diagram of the heart and learn how to take your pulse.

KidsHealth: Your Heart & Circulatory System
kidshealth.org/kid/htbw/heart.html
Learn about the heart and blood flow, and watch a video of a person getting an EKG to check their heart health.

Texas Heart Institute: Project Heart for Kids: Fun Facts
www.texasheart.org/ProjectHeart/Kids/Learn/fun_facts.cfm
Fun facts and quizzes about the heart, blood, circulatory system, and more, from the Texas Heart Institute.

Every effort has been made to ensure that these websites are appropriate for children. However, because of the nature of the Internet, it is impossible to guarantee that these sites will remain active indefinitely or that their contents will not be altered.